I0422389

Sommario

4

1. The ideal Company

The ideal society that comes after the peasant company then after the industrial one must not be more founded on the work but founded on The Love how and why: first of all it must be guaranteed a minimum wage but vital to all, that is that with this money a person can live in dignity.

Decrease the working hours by 4 hours per day for 5 days but let everyone work, except housewives and chronic and handicapped patients.

Those who want to work more hours is free to do so by taking more money for every hour done in more than 4 hours required, also choosing to do the extra hours another job that likes the most. The work only 4 hours is to make life more livable especially for public and private employees, as for example the workers of the industry that of crafts and farmers.

The private property will always have to exist, because that is the spring for progress, indeed it will have to be increased, reducing the state in a form of guardian and manager of public money derived from taxes imposed.

The company founded on The Love will have to be a limitation of weapons to those who do not necessarily need it and not give it to everyone.

Another thing to do is not to show on television scenes where there is violence especially with weapons, in order to avoid a simulation especially in minors.

In movies with scenes of violence must be forbidden to enter until one is over 18s. In school, a subject must be inserted that teaches love and respect for other people, this up to being over 18s. Always at school there must be a subject that teaches to love All living beings of the planet, from animals to trees and herbs and insects etc. etc.

In schools it will have to be rewarded in addition to those who behave well, giving him money or other ways.

Rewarding the good in all its forms is tantamount to building a society with less violence and fewer murders. A company created on The Love is not so easy to do it, but if people teach it from the small to love everything that surrounds us surely we will have a society less violent, but based more on Love. I can no longer hear the news daily, with deaths or violence on women or minors treated badly even by their peers, and I think that much guilt has television.

We must first of all restore trust among the citizens, now locked in their homes with a thousand locks, to return that brotherhood that existed In the peasant civilization where whole families met in the evening after a whole day of work, they worked all day together to do before or work the earth and then also by chance to be in the company to say two mocks to train the toils of work and spend time in cheerfulness.

Today that time and now past, everyone to do their own work in silence as there exists in the factories the chain work, which reaches the limit of madness.

Because we only work 4 hours, because we are not machines,

but we are people and we have the right to enjoy life since we have only one and it is not very long. Enjoying life day after day is the true goal of the Society of Love.

For those who do not respect the law there will be no longer the prison but the community that help him to learn a craft that would serve after discounted the penalty on the return in society, life sentences will also be abolished, but it will be discounted on the basis of the conduct of the detainee in the community until it is held appropriate by the court for its return to society. In the community will be taught almost all trades, from agriculture to all trades useful for living.

Life must be a joy to be in the world and not all locked up in offices or factories and shops etc.

etc. Without enjoying what is most beautiful in the world, do what you want to do, I for example in my hobby or created more than 1200 giant sequoias and other sunrises I, just because they are endangered trees, this I Has Given more satisfaction that all years spent in the factory to work, this is because I decided to decide it, and not imposed by others even if paid with a salary.

Knows To How many people would like to work only 4 hours and with That you can span family, and the hours that remain free devote themselves to what you like most.

The time is ripe for what happens the work only 4 hours, because today there are so many people who do not Has Work, then there are also a multitude of refugees who can work the other 4 hours of missing work so you can have a better life for everyone. In my opinion it is useless to make a super more production, because first there is a difficulty in selling the product, second in planet Earth can not withstand a super consumerism, because even if it does not seem everything we consume comes from the Earth, and the planet before or Then it will go on tilt if consumerism is exaggerated. I already think about it, and if everyone in this world as it exists from us that every person in your car we have all who knows if the trees will make it absorb all the exhaust gases of the motor vehicles and Turn them into oxygen or they won't make it anymore? In my opinion they will not make it any more to transform them, then always from my point of view should be reduced to the maximum the cut of the trees, in order to avoid a tomorrow the lack of oxygen made by the trees. Because so much is assumed that in a future all will has a car, new or used that is, and pollution if not found another fuel that is not oil, the pollution will be global. So the problem is: work less but work all, then do not make the super production especially of cars, because they are the ones that pollute more.

The Society of Loving you as if we were all brothers, will have to be as social as possible to help where there is need of the state understood as if it were a great tribe where all and social for the sake of all the members of the tribe, the aid of the state to all the people who They need: Who of a house, who needs to work, who needs assistance because he has given birth or because he is handicapped both physical and mental, but do it by private or cooperative companies.

The state will have to deal directly with schools and hospitals and communities of recovery of prisoners who have broken the law, the rest will have to take care of private companies, how to build houses for those who do not have, roads, assistance to those who need it etc. but the All financed by the state with taxes imposed.

To love you as it happens in a tribe, that is the true love, to feel brothers with each other, a great tribe a state that loves its citizens and also the refugees of other States, in worrying to find a job and a house at all.

This is the true society of love.

2. *Love for All*

The Love, the most beautiful thing God has invented, wanting well more than as brothers in a couple of husband and wife, suffer when your companion suffers, or rejoice together when things go well, this is the beauty of love. And when the heart is open to love, one loves everyone as we are all brothers, this is what God has given us, this is precisely what gave us the power to love all.

We hope that in the near future this becomes the behavior of man with other men, and stop making wars, the ugliest thing that man has invented.

Love, this small word but with a great power, the power to open the heart to all indiscriminately, from the mighty men of the Earth to the last of the tramps, ready to love even a little floret created by God, just Only a second in the dwelling to look at it to understand the strength of this word love, love for all, from the tramps to the last floret of the world.

This is what God has taught us, to love all from the first to the last, which can also be the last floret of the Earth. Love this word that when it is sincere in your heart opens all the doors of the world, even the most difficult.

3. *I love*

Who I am, I'm just crazy with a lot of certificate, but I love, I love the life of every living thing, from Sequoia to Violet, from the whale to the smallest of the minnows, from the elephant to the smallest of the kittens, but I love more than all my wife and my family, this is the most beautiful gift God has made to me. I also love the trees so majestic and beautiful but so fragile under the chainsaw of Man, then I love everything there is in this planet that God has given us, and we men we everything that comes back comfortable from the times without thinking the damage that is done against this Planet.

My greatest love goes to my wife who wants me so well and I

return because I am very much in love.

Love that I also feel for my family and friends and so much and I wish to All to live well and healthy This is what matters most, you own health is what matters, I lost it I was only 28 years old and since ' now I am no longer healed. My illness is called bipolar mood syndrome or as it was called once psychosis depressive maniac, ugly name but unfortunately it is touched to me and I can not do anything out that take the medicine and heal me.

4. *His Holiness Pope Francis*

The Pope this great Pope who gave us God.

His Holiness Pope Francis is a man who with his simplicity has bought all Christians and perhaps even more than all Christians, for his simplicity and love for all those who are willing to love the neighbor just as he did Saint Francis love all with great simplicity. This is a true Pope, Pope of all those who in the world want to feel loved, and love them themselves.

The Pope with his answer to everyone, to those who need comfort, also a call rekindles the desire to live, to live in the hope of a better afterlife than this.

The Pope in his choosing a simple life without riches, teaches us all to live in a simple way, to give more love to everyone especially to those who have been more unfortunate than us in health and suffers every day.

I pray for the pope who camps so much and in good health, because if he deserves to live a lot, and teaches us even more to love the neighbor, either this a person or the nature that surrounds us.

I love this pope because it is always against the wars that bring only destruction and death even innocent children of what is going on

5. *Love the Sun*

- Love the world, because and our house.
- Love the Earth, because it feeds us.
- Loving the sea, because with its fish and its warmth distributed on the planet, it makes a pleasant climate and with many variations from the heat to the cold.
- Loving the trees, which give us so much oxygen and wood to heat our homes, also give us the wood to build the houses and wood to build our furniture.
- Love water, because it gives life to all living beings on the planet.
- Love fire, because it warms the houses and keeps us company.
- Love the air, because you can breathe and so live and also

because moves with the wind the clouds that bring the rain that gives life to the Earth.

- Love animals, who feed us or keep us company, like dogs or cats and other animals still.
- Love the fish, who feed us with their good flesh and also because they keep us company in the Aquaria and the seas.
- To love the Sun, which of God is the imagination, to love the sun that with water gives life to the whole world and enlightens us the day from the night, with all the wonders of this planet Earth.

6. *Why Jesus*

Because Jesus, because Jesus, because Jesus, the brain I got sick of such a bad illness, that in the morning it throws me so down in the mood that you do not make it to do anything and you are so badly with the thoughts of wanting to die, and it is so every morning, never passes.

What is beautiful about this disease that taught me to love, to love all that is beautiful to love, people especially the nature, so weak and fragile, but so sweet to love all its varieties of animals, plants, and insects etc. etc.

When I start this disease that came to me acute psychosis, I was all day struggling with God and the devil. God who grumbled me that I was naughty, and the devil who terrified me all day, or how I was hurting the hard thing several days, until I caught Serenase that I reassure immediately Letting me have a good night's sleep after months of sleeping very little.

These memories do not go away from the mind, I still remember all the acute psychosis as I had happened yesterday, instead have passed 20 years, but with the mood to feel cheerful or sad of this I still suffer, with the morning funeral and the afternoon quite Quiet and so always.

7. *Writing is nice*

It's nice to write, freely write everything that goes through your head, without decency without anyone criticizing you if you write right or wrong that it is, this is the real freedom, you can publish your thoughts, and as long as there will be the freedom , the freedom to write without someone giving you the title of a theme to play, or an article of some newspaper, in short be free to choose to write what you like best to let others know; But, I'm crazy without a bridle, without someone muzzling me, and it's so nice to be free.

I invite all the people of the world to be free, free to say their own opinion about what is most at heart, and if they can do it freely means that in that country there is freedom, but if they can not do it freely means that There is a dictatorship in that country. Then you have to go to another state where you can write your own thoughts freely, and denounce by writing what happens in the state of which we have gone away.

I invite everyone to write, even a small booklet of what is wrong, and must be changed, not to demolish a state but to make it better than it is now, and make it more enjoyable to live there.

However, you write and leave a memory of you.

8. *In my illness I learned to love*

This tremendous disease that terrified me for 3 months, has left me a gift to love, to love everything that is good on this planet, and I with my criticisms I try to improve it, even if I do not know whether it is right yes or not.

I fell in love with everything that's good on the planet, to regain from all the nature to the people, like my wife and my little girls, and all family members of both my family and my wife, then I love all the good people especially this Pope FRANCES CO that his humility filled me with the heart of joy.

This disease has taught me to love the weakest beings both people and in nature, such as the handicapped both physical and mental, and also of nature the More vulnerable weaker beings like trees, which offer us so much especially oxygen, a precious commodity that we forget that plants give us free as long as we love them.

Unfortunately even among the plants there are many diseases that endanger entire forests like that of chestnut, here from us in Casentino. And that is why I strive to say that the more forest is varied and the more difficult the plants will become ill.

9. Love your Neighbor

To love people of whatever state they are, to offer them a legal work not to black, to respect them as human persons of any religion are, this is the true democratic freedom of a nation, to offer legal work to all refugees of any state be, this It is the maximum of a civilization that is defined democratic. To welcome even handicapped people from other countries in their country and offer them the care they need even if they do not have money, this is a great gesture of civilization of a democratic state.

Helping everyone without making wars to bring so you say peace, in fact you kill people and enough even if to die are more soldiers than civilians are still human people, and not plastic fool. You soldier or cop from those who get the order to shoot your fellow even of another nation that is not yours, do not shoot because a person is always worth more than a bullet of lead is of any rifle was fired, if you love to life never shoot.

Do not make my usual mistake that I went hunting and shooting at free animals in nature, innocent because they had not committed any crime if not the gift of living, were innocent and shot killing them the freedom to live.

What a big pity I did, I regret so much of what I did to nature. And so you soldier or cop that you're never shooting anyone and then regret one day when you realize what you're doing.

10. *The difficult life of a mentally handicapped*

Living a life with a mental handicap is difficult the only force to go forward is the love that is given to you by the family, especially for those who are married by their wife. From The Times my wife gets mad a little with me, and at almost always right she telling me that I am a text one that does not change ideas, but unfortunately that I can do is done so, and change is difficult.

I want so much good to my wife, who helped me in all these years of sickness giving me the strength to go on with life even in the worst moments when I attempted suicide for three times, was she to save me taking me to the hospital , I owe her life.

The time has passed though and it is not that it is so good, yet I take Strong depression crisis especially in the morning I'm very bad, hopefully you find the right medicine this is my hope.

I'm so fat I don't know I will weigh on 180 pounds, the two of my daughters get mad at me when they see I eat too much, they do so because they love me and the regret to have a father so fat that he does not make it to budge, you have to give more straight to the two of my fig Lie and my wife telling me a hundred times to eat less.

11. *The word Love*

Loving, loving, this word with a thousand combinations, there are those who love good food, the pleasure of eating well at the table.

Love sports, football or Formula One, or other sports, volleyball, athletics, in short, all the sports that exist.

Love the work that one does, have pleasure in doing it.

Love animals of any kind, or love a dog or a cat, or other animals such as horses etc. etc.

Love the weakest beings like trees and all plants even those from flower.

Love the flowers from the most fragrant and beautiful, up to the smallest of the floret. Love fish both in nature and in aquariums.

Love. Love, this word so short but that it can open a thousand hearts, for Every passion that one has, but the most important is to love the people of any state or religion are, or, to love Jesus, what they have written of him as the gospel and thus to make himself a friar or nun or priest.

Love women, or men of the same sex. When a man loves a woman only but to make us sex and just or vice versa, or as I like it, love my wife who gave me so much, two beautiful little girls, love my wife every day, for what she does at home and how she cares for my little girls and because of my Wife I'm in love, so much.

However, the most important thing is to love every living being, but it is not enough to love the Earth, the water, the fire and any soil or stone exists on our planet Earth, because even a stone is used to build your home.

12. The love I have for plants

I do not know from the times I can not think of anything to write but the brain is done so, from the times to mind a hundred things to write and then from the Times nothing, but it is so and there I do nothing.

But I'll try to say something for example I still have two hundred sequoias to give more I also have other plants to give, but hopefully you find it to give away, many of these trees are endangered, they are my puppies these trees and I care that they do not dry out , or throw them away, I wish they lived all but it is not as easy as to say, because if not gifts to those who love plants, people take it because they are free plant them and then do not water them even and so in the summer they dry and pouf there are no longer , so much effort to Nothing. The plants you have to give to those who love them really, are like puppies that if you love them they grow well, if not grow up and sickly.

But still you have to have confidence in people and hope they love them. Sometimes some plant dries up to me and I regret a lot I'm really sick, and so I will not sow them anymore because first of all it is not easy to find to give them and then also because if someone dries I'm like or already said so much bad.

13. *The welfare of a people*

I do not know how the state measures the welfare of its people, if it goes according to how many things one owns, motorcycles, cars, land, houses or apartments, money, in short from how much wealth one owns, if it is a worker than it takes as salary, I do not know how to calculate the Goodies King of their own people.

For me the wellbeing of a person is measured in a salary that one can decently span his family, from the work he does if he likes, or is forced to do so to span his family. See the work that one does, whether it is a tiring job, or a work done in the chain, or a dangerous job. See even if it is a worker if it owns the house or an apartment.

In short, to measure the Wellness you have to see also how many hours of freedom it has, and how many hours of work it has to do to take a good salary. I do not know how to calculate this welfare of a person, but I think that the best life for a person is to work less than the current 8 hours but work 4 hours a day taking the usual salary and can choose from if, if do more hours of work , or dedicate free time to stay more in the family, or create hobbies that like to do, in short, in my opinion the wellbeing of an individual is of how happy it is to stay in the world, and the possibility of working less hours is definitely an addition to being happy.

Then with the unemployment that is there today and the emigration of the peoples where there are wars to our country, it is not difficult to find the manpower to work all 4 hours with the usual salary since in Germany salaries for a worker are twice the Salary of An Italian in Italy.

In short, for me the wellbeing of an individual is also how much I can enjoy life day after day, and no stay all day closed inside a building to work.

14. *Pollution*

The pollution in the near future will increase for sure, and be very dangerous to human health, especially if to pollute will be the air we breathe every day and the water we drink from the cinnamon, you have to do something and just before you spend the time and both Too late.

With the gas of the heating and the exhaust gases of cars, the air pollution in the future will increase for sure, hopefully the trees will make it absorb all the carbon dioxide produced in super quantity produced as I said before by Heating of the dwellings, whatever the burnt product, and by the gas of any engine it is.

Another problem is the

pollution of the water that with the abusive landfills the poison of the waste ends all under ground and goes to pollute All aquifers, but hopefully well.

But poor world in what hand are you, instead of respecting you because you are our home, we pollute you with all the cartwheel possible and unimaginable, you world that offer life to all you do not come respected for nothing and that I regret, I that I have as a car an old one of twenty Years throw it away does not seem right because it still goes, and as long as I will keep it, also because it was my father and it is an emotional memory, it is among the first cars that made gasoline green, and has the engine Fire, an excellent engine, consumes a little 17 km with a liter, it is not bad for a car of twenty-one years ago.

15. *Lamberto*

Lamberto, my best friend, we have been friends since I was fourteen, now I have forty-eight and we are always friends.

Both lovers of plants, he likes more than all the Araucaria Araucana to me the Giant sequoia he was also to see them in California and told me that they are gigantic redwoods.

Lamberto is a kind of weird as I am, but he is normal and I'm not. He had put on a plant nursery near my house, but the business did not go well so Has Closed the nursery.

My friend called with the nickname Lambi is very good, had a job at the Tuscany region but did not like it much because he did not feel free, so he got fired and came here in Casentino where he has the house and put on this nursery , he likes the freedom to do what he seems to be Without being commanded by anyone.

I have known him for so many years is a good and talented person, we hope to remain friends for life this would be the most beautiful thing of all.

Lambi loves all nature as I love him, he knows so many wild herbs to eat and makes some yummy salads, it goes now I salute Lamberto and hope to be friends forever.

16. *My conscience*

But I do not know if my living in this world is served to something, either good or done or something bad that I did, living a life so to wonder if with my craft of carpenter brought only harm to my planet and I was just a machine system Consumerist that reigns in this world, we hope that consumerism does not lead us to the ecological destruction of the whole planet, with the disappearance of many animal or plant species or fish existing on the planet.

This question to what I have served I do not know, but I torture the conscience of having mistaken in working so much wood for human pleasure.

I do not know if then it serves

something all this exaggerated consumerism, in changing the face of our land to the pleasure of man and enough.

Something should be done to Restore the ecological damage done, as long as we still in time hoping not to get too late.

But my conscience still bites me, because you see on television that the ecological restoration if they care all highly, they think all of the money and nature who cares, we destroy our home the world and we think all of the money, so it's not good, you have to States all over the world agree, to stop making wars and think a little more about the world in which you live, to restore the damage done to nature.

17. *Three hundred deaths for freedom*

Today Thursday, October 3, 2013 were found drowned at sea in the beaches of Lampedusa more than three hundred people drowned in the sea, they ran away from the wars and hunger that is in their countries, and year found death a hundred meters on arrival from the promised meta as a dream of a welcoming and wealthy country.

But it is not so, often exploited because clandestine find themselves to do the worst jobs, or to peddle drugs or to make prostitutes, or the arms to work in the fields to a misery, this is the end of the beautiful dream of a free country where you can feel good , as I feel bad in knowing all this, escape from a tragedy to end it in another.

However these three hundred deaths must make us think, that the wars and the Hunger in the world must be ceased all we have the right to live in your own country in a system worthy of human beings, without wars without hunger, this should be the first law of every state of the world, will be good to its people, create schools streets houses , this and more will be good for their people, and no buy tanks warships ready to be flaked against their own people if they do not obey taxes and laws imposed by their own rulers.

However remember that on 3 October 2013 more than three hundred people died for the pursuit of freedom.

And so it's not fair.

18. *Thank you God*

Because God took me to the best part of my body the brain (manic depressive psychosis) and I made him sick, I know that with this disease you have taught me to love all the living beings of this planet, but not only have you taught me also to love the Earth the water The fire, and even the stones with which we build our homes.

But I remember that when I raved about the struggle between God and the devil I had in my brain was so strong the psychic pain I had in my head.

The struggle between good and evil that existed in my brain, fortunately to win this fight was good, and that is how I learned to love all that is good in this planet, thank you God that you taught me to love , though I am very ill because of the depression that I Especially in the morning that I get up with a funeral mood that makes me feel so bad with the desire to die that leaves me no more space in the mind, I thank you equally God because in the illness I taught me to love, a love so strong for all living beings and also as the land that is what gives me the strength to be still alive.

I thank God for this disease that makes me rejoice even when I see a little floret, and you gave me a wonderful wife that I love so much.

Thank you God

19. *Racism*

Racism, what a bad word especially when you live it on your own skin, be guilty only because you are coming from another place also of your own state, south and north, East West, East West, so you divide the world. But it is ugly who holds this grudge in the heart, in the Society of love this word must be abolished, because it hurts both and those who are racist and the one who undergoes racism.

I am married to a beautiful woman, but it is the countries of Eastern Europe, and I see that in my family not everyone has accepted it of good degree and this makes me tar badly and also she is hurt. From my wife's family they welcomed me as a son, and they love me so much, the thing that bothered me most is that my sister didn't come to my church wedding, it didn't come because otherwise she lost two Days at sea in a bungalow, this is the thing that gave me more displeasure than anything.

However I love my wife a lot and I am sorry for those who are racist, because in his soul must suffer a lot, hating others just because they come from other places, even their own state. Times behind was poorly seen who came from southern Italy and came to the north to work, they were called Southerner, but they were all good people, they did humble works that did not want to do those of northern Italy.

20. *The War*

Wars, that ugly invention weapons, but not only weapons but do also punch against another person, but not only to punch but also quarrel against a person, but quarreling in the family is even more ugly. I when my wife gets angry at me, I'm so sick, but bad, bad, when you get angry my wife does so: stop talking to me and I'm hurt to know that a person is with me, especially if family. I'm sick of knowing if someone is with me, let alone make wars people like they must be sick, kill people equal to you, to destroy houses that for them a family puts a life.

We think of the terror that a person lives inside, feel the bombs near you, the machine gun bursts towards you, must be Terrifying to live all this for one person.

For this then whole families flee from these nations and seek peace in other countries.

This is why the nations where these refugees arrive must welcome them in the best possible way, because they escape from a terrifying place, and it is bad to live like that.

In society founded on Love, the small army that must serve only for the purpose of defending one's nation and nothing more.

21. *The Peace*

Peace that beautiful word, but no because it is a word, but when it really exists among people, among peoples, but the most beautiful peace is when there is in a family, when there is love among the family.

Peace for people with more weapons think of bringing it to other states with war, and it is not so peace leads with love and that is how true peace is created.

Even among the peoples so different from each other when they make the war that terrifies all their citizens would not be nicer to put themselves at a table and clarify their views on what is wrong that does not go between the two peoples, and solve them by voice their own dissensions.

I do not know why peace is so beautiful to go to ruin with war, the destruction of its buildings the dead that are there when you make wars, what a sad war.

Peace instead is the construction of something beautiful, to solve the problems of its citizens, to make them participate in the construction of their own peace with the other neighboring states and with the whole world, this would be the most beautiful thing that exists, a world of peace, where everyone is They love the countries of the south with those of the north, the countries of the West with those of the east, get there with the words to create this.

Words yes but words of love.

22. *The weapons*

If you create a weapon is not to give life to anyone, but to take away the life of any living being exists on Earth, even if you use it to defend and shoot against the enemy, it is always to take away the life of someone, right or wrong that is never use a weapon If you don't want to regret it after killing anyone, man or animal it is.

If it were for me I would stop building the weapons, especially those so called Read, guns and rifles, they are the ones that kill more civilians than all, and it is not right that it is.

War helicopters, airplanes, tanks, submarines, warships, aircraft carriers, launches missiles, machine guns, rifles, pistols, hand grenades, bazuca, anti-tank bombs, depleted uranium bombs, atomic bombs etc. etc. all weapons to kill more Possible people and it's not fair that it's So.

And peace out that love that weapons have you ever wondered? It is precisely so that the weapon of peace is love.

Instead of creating a world where there is peace and love we continue to create more and more destructive weapons, hoping that some state will buy them and operate them and then sell them ammunition, and so the chain no longer ends. Changing this system is difficult to run too much money and power behind it, but in our little we try to say no to the weapons so called Read and so one step forward we will have done, meanwhile the life of many animals we have saved it, and also that of many Civilians we will have saved it, and it is a small step towards peace and love.

23. *Thanks to my parents*

Thank you Jesus, who gave me a father and a mother who loved me and raised me with good principles and with the lead compared to the others of any state come and any age have.

My father and mother gave us a job and a house for one to us two brothers and a sister, they gave us a road in work at all three, thank you mom thank you father, the work went well and in life we were able to renovate the houses left by our Parents.

It's been a few years since my dad died he wanted us to all three so well, hopefully he's in heaven because he was so good and loved everyone. Now there is my mother, we are three brothers and we want all three so well, pity that my mother has come a slight stroke and does not walk Very well, I regret so much anyway we never leave her alone, in turn we go to find her.

Thank you parents for all that you have done for us and especially because you have put us in the world and you have grown up without ever letting us miss anything and why you have wanted us so well.

To me when I came to this depressive manic illness My father took me with the car around to make me entertain and thanks to him that I immediately recovered from the delirium I had, thanks also to the medicines that I have always taken from the hour.

24. My brothers

Wanting well with all the people, but above all among the family is important to want well, even if sometimes the accounts do not come back it is good to clarify immediately and go back to wanting as well as before, because to bring the grudge among the family you are sick in the spirit and just , wanting well in the family among siblings is the most beautiful thing in the world.

I love my brothers so much, and if I was the only son I will be sad I would miss the affection of my brothers, my brother who is a little older and I love him so much, and my sister that she too is a little older than me , but you want so much good with her too. I call them Big

Brother and sister only because they are a little older than me, but the biggest and most weight I am.

The chief who manages everything is mine Sister, she keeps the accounts of everything and is very good and honest.

All three brothers want so much good to our mother, who is now in poor shape because she had a stroke that does not make her walk so well. My dad died a few years, he was very good and generous too.

In short we are a beautiful family and I am glad that it is so, especially because you want so much good, it is a good thing to want well.

25. *A planet founded on hatred*

A planet founded on hatred over those who have more than necessary, be racist and create discord among other peoples and then sell weapons and ammunition in exchange for oil or gas as methane.

Create wars among peoples, or civil wars just for the simple purpose of selling weapons in exchange for raw materials, such as timber precious stones or uranium or other things that serve the richest nations of technology. This richness of the so-called rich countries, someone has to put us back and So The poorest countries are cool of their goods in exchange for weapons to make war to neighboring countries.

But wars are not the only thing for a world where hatred is, racism is another thing that increases hatred among peoples and among people, Feeling superior to others as it happens even in school bullying, or in the life of youth when they do the manifestations there are always those ready to make confusion and crack or fire everything. Hatred is also when a person owns many houses or factories and is envied by those who have nothing or bad business.

However one thing is certain hatred and evil in the world, the important is to marginal these people and to think that peace and love always win on evil.

26. *Elderly people*

Older people are like children in need of affection and love, rich in the experience of living life are open book encyclopedias. The elderly people who teach us the whole experience to cook, and live an honest life without sins. When they are older and there are some ailment, they teach us to love what life is, because one day we will also have this experience and we hope that there is someone to love us and take care of ourselves.

The old people left alone are tender, with those eyes looking for someone to exchange two words to get out of that silence forced by the loneliness in which they live.

The elders who teach us the tricks and values of life and the true secrets of living well and in harmony with others, and who is married teaches us how to want Good for all your life, and when you give a basin between if you son fill you with the heart of joy in seeing that in so many years there is still the affection and the joy of living together.

Unfortunately, the elderly often find themselves together in the hospices, a kind of forced prison because in the family they had no time to take care of them, or because they are sick too badly that they need so much care.

27. The most beautiful thing in the world is peace

Jesus, because it gives us a planet so beautiful that I define the earthly paradise, we deserve it yes or No. I don't know if we deserve it, I have strong doubts because man continues to plunder all that is good to consume, regardless of no species, animal and vegetable We hope a day of non-regret and the ugliest thing is that not in regard even for if same Or, with wars and murders.

With its immense technology the man has come to build planes that carry the bombs without the need of the pilot, all to kill as many people as possible without the risk of the pilot dying.

There is so much hatred among the peoples that in the world there are always wars, When you understand the man who with the wars you do not get nothing but destruction of houses and deaths.

Let us all pray together with one's own religion that one day will take place a miracle, that in the world there is peace and love among all peoples and no more wars and deaths for human stupidity.

Peace among peoples is the most beautiful thing that can exist.

28. *The Tramps*

The tramps the innocent eyes of society, that when a society is healthy the bums are helped and do not exist, instead when a state does not think of them is a sick society and the state thinks only for itself and not to the poorest. The tramps the innocent eyes of Jesus, who evaluate the love that is in a state or the selfishness that exists among the rulers, ready not to spend a penny for the poor.

The Tramps the most tender part of a society, should be helped give him a home if they make it to work give him even a job as simple as a sweeper or other, very often suffer from a mental illness like depression or some other disease. But it is from them that you see if a society is healthy or not, or is a selfish society and that's it.

In the Society of love that I have in my mind, they are in the first place to be helped because the poor in a democratic state that is defined as such, the poor should not exist. But the poor are not only homeless but also pensioners with the least pension, the chronic sick of any disease exists, and refugees fleeing from wars or poverty try to respond to this request for help by offering him a job even humble , this would be the true society of love, offering help to the most needy help would even new jobs to help others.

29. *death*

Today Friday, October 25, 2013 I went at 11.30 hours from my mother to the hospital and I found her that she was behaving, but what made me more effect is an elderly woman who is in the bed in front of my mum. In the day ahead this woman breathed with the mask of oxygen, not a word to give a sign of life nothing said nothing just breathing. Today when I went to the hospital this old woman moaning but slightly, the breath had made itself more wheezing, or rang the bell to call a nurse who came right away, watched her and with her head made me sign no, with that sign or understood that ER Near his death, after a short time the breath became weaker and at a much slower pace, he breathed slowly.

At this point I had already given From eating to my mum, clean the cutlery and the denture and or given a basin to my mum greeted him and I came away, I think that old person died after a short time; But what has made me more effect is the loneliness that wax around this woman, no relative no friend, alone remained alone in the face of death.

What a bad thing the loneliness, what a bad death, we hope that it does not touch me a death like that.

30. *Dedicated to You*

I dedicate this to my thoughts to those who are never happy with what he has, but always wants more than others and never satiate, more houses more land more power more money and is never happy.

I dedicate my thoughts to the miseries that put aside as much money as possible and are never happy, and are concerned to make the expenses for themselves.

I dedicate this my thoughts to the selfish who also want the things that they expect at the atria, dragging for this even the people in court.

I dedicate this my thoughts to those who have ever more thirst for power than ever enough and want to command on all and often to have more power to be at war with near States or even against its own people.

I dedicate my thought to the envious who always escapes him from the Eyes what others have and often they also speak badly.

I dedicate this my thoughts to all the workers who work honestly and do not have thirst for power, are not misery nor selfish and even jealous, but they are satisfied with the salary they have and make a life humble but honest and with their work they make rich all their own population.

31. *Thanks Roberto, thank you Giacomo*

Thank you Roberto, thanks James, for all you do for others, without asking a penny money, but only to give love to those who need urgent care, once again thank you.

You are two volunteers of mercy and this makes you a great honor and I am very happy to be your uncle, good guys there is no greater thing than to give help to those who need urgent care and help. Continue this is the most beautiful thing in the world and you are part of it, and never tire of what you do for others, because that makes you great for both men and for God.

Giving help to those who need makes people of heroes,

without a rifle or a gun, but only the will to give love and help those in need. Thank you Also to the other volunteers who like you for free help people that year need urgent help, and you are ready to give him a hand.

Another thank you goes to all those people who free help people to a decent life even if they are sick of any illness it is but they do not make it more alone and year by force need help. A thank you also goes to my brother and sister, that you are busy before my father who had a disease called Pick disease, which invalidated him to stay in bed until death, and now deal with my mother who had a slight stroke and does not make it More alone but needs help.

A Thanks to all these people.

32. *The school, the Love*

The school the place where people of the future are created, where a person opens to learn the life that awaits him in the future, is helped by the teachers to understand what is good or bad in life. The school should teach how to behave towards the other people and the environment in which we live, to respect above all the nature in all its forms animals plants insects reptiles etc. and to respect above all the land in which we live and Condemn those who want to pollute it with any waste or used chemicals that can harm the environment in which we live.

In the school there should be an hour a week where you teach to love, just explain what is love, love for people, love for all living beings, and encourage the good so that in the future we will have a society Of more good people and thus we shall defeat the wars among the peoples that so badly do to people.

Building a civilization of good people in school should be the goal of every nation in the world, to encourage good is not to improve the society in which we live. To open the heart to love and respect all people, to love nature and the earth and to respect it from a small age can only bring that well-being in the society in which we live.

Today to bring this teaching makes it the religion, but in my opinion there should be just an hour as teaching also made by the professors suitable for this matter of education.

33. *The poverty of a people*

I dedicate my thoughts to the poor, but not to the poor of distant continents but to the poor who are here in Italy, the poor who ask for alms on the street to those who eat go where lunch is offered for free, and to sleep they go in the public dormitories Or at the train station or under the bridges covered with cartoons and newspapers to shelter from the cold winter.

But there are other poor ones who have a minimum pension and the unemployed, who do not make it to pay the rent and the bills which are light water and gas or pay these or buy food and medicines This is the real poverty of the Italians.

And who is the government

does not think, or pretends not to understand that instead the true Wealth is going to pay more workers that will consume more and more work for everyone and so more well-being for everyone. It is useless to give more money to companies because that money will not create widespread wellbeing but will only serve to enrich those industrials to which they touch that money, and the problem once spent all the money comes back from the end.

Poverty that ugly thing you are no longer master to buy what you like, but often for so many people can not buy even the necessary this is the ugly of poverty.

34. The Rich

Who are the rich in Italy?

The rich in Italy are those who have a job dependent or in their own that Has The luck of working because here every day they close factories and shops, but the real wealthy are those who govern us, politicians who wage themselves without anyone who protests for the exaggerated wages that you make.

The rich are also those industrialists who are in contact with politicians and make them win public works contracts.

The wealthy who enjoy making fun of the poor by buying Cars of luxury, or with the Pharaohs villas in Italy and abroad or when they go to the sea have colossal boats moored in the ports, ready always starting to make a turn in the high seas.

The rich have always existed, who has more than others there has always been since the pharaohs in Egypt until the present day, but the unjust is not what there are the rich but when wealth is enclosed in few hands few people this is the true injustice, wealth must be spread even to the workers , so you create a rich and working company for everyone.

The workers who with their work give food to all rich and poor, these are the true heroes of a democratic nation.

35. *The water*

Water, to this precious good is often not given the right value but without it there would be no life on earth, often polluted because rivers are used as sewers to open sky, pollute the aquifers with abusive landfills and also throw at sea the Radioactive waste of nuclear power plants.

All this is not good because, by watering the fields by taking the waters from the ditches or from the rivers, this pollution we find in our food or in the one dedicated to animals.

Water, which when it rains much creates damage to man's buildings, however if there was no water there would be the desert and it would be worse forces.

Water, in the house that comfort, especially when it is drunk that going to cinnamon you drink some nice Glass, maybe cool, or to shower in the house a comfort that in ancient times did not exist. And then with the water in the house there are also machines like the washing machine and the dishwasher that help the Massie in his daily work.

In short, the water has a thousand uses and you have to be careful not to waste it needlessly because as long as there is water there is life on the whole Earth, without water there is the desert and desolation.

36. The fire

The fire, this element that we find in nature often caused by lightning or gas emanating from the ground naturally, has accompanied the man since the antiquity that served both to cook the meat and to warm up as we do still today especially In country houses.

This precious element for man is sometimes used unjustly to fire the woods, causing enormous damage to nature.

In other parts of the world it is used as a renewal of pastures for livestock, or to create new ones, giving fire to the forest.

The fire if used wisely is a great friend of man, you can use it to melt the metals and work them smoothly, you can melt the glass to give it shape, and so for many other useful functions.

There are different types of fire, the first one that comes to mind is that generated by wood, another type of fire is that generated by gases, methane, LPG and others, another fire is that generated by oil and derivatives, another is the one released by the fossil carbon , in short, there are different types of fuel that man Has Discovered in nature, however if these fires are not used wisely they can cause considerable damage.

37. *Things that make me feel bad*

I am a poor madman because I would like to change the vision that man has of the world, to regain the environment in which we live that man does not respect at all, these days it was discovered that in Campania were buried radioactive waste of scraps of Nuclear power plants of other states that have now polluted soil and aquifers, so much so that they were born deformed animals like goats grazing in that area, the buffaloes that grazed and drank water of that area made radioactive milk, so the buffalo Mozzarella of Campania have forbidden to do it.

And I like a simpleton on these things I'm sick because when there's no respect for the environment in which we live to me are things that make me feel very Bad.

Another thing that I do not want is that the woods are made all in forestry for large plots of land and without reinserting species of trees that once, before he put his hands on the man, wax and so we lose the diversity of trees important not so much for men or but by nature itself destroying all the microhabitat that was caused by those trees now missing. And when I talk about the environment badly treated by man, I'm very sick.

Another thing that makes me sick is the respect for human and animal life that man does not have at all, so much is that wars are done destroying everything, human lives and buildings and often commit murders of relatives or friends; You go hunting for protected animals bringing them near the extinction, these are things that for a mentally ill make him feel very bad but bad, bad.

I would like in stead a society where the good and the love for everything that exists on this planet in the center.

38. *The hunt*

Jesus forgive me I made the greatest sin that a man can do, without reflecting on the damage I did, I killed free animals in nature poor birds, because I was hunting especially of blackbirds, acorns and some pheasant.

Poor beasts were free in nature without defense but with the only means of defense that was the escape.

Poor animals kill them without needing to eat is the biggest sin that a man can do, I regret so much, exchanging a sport, as it is called, for the useless killing of free animals in nature, what a big shame I did Unwittingly, that God and nature forgive me.

I do not intend to defend

myself from this sin, however, more than killing these animals I liked More long walks than I did in the woods and meadows.

Hunting that stupid sport, apart from hunting wild boar, of which there are many, the rest is just a useless killing of free animals in nature, and it is a big shame that the man has not understood or does not want to understand.

Loving the nature that surrounds us is what man should do, not kill animals needlessly.

Poor beasts hope that God and nature forgive me.

39. *The forest*

The forestry the most beautiful body of the Italian state, defending nature from those who mistreats contaminated it or those who fire the woods or those who do not respect the laws on hunting, in short to defend all nature in Italy.

If I go back in the years I would like to be part of this body of the forest I find the most beautiful job of all the work that man can do, defend nature from those who mistreats, contaminated it or those who fire the woods or those who go hunting and do not respect Laws that protect some animals.

The forestry this body so precious that I think is not valued enough and in stead in my opinion is the most precious of all the other bodies of the Italian state.

The forest these people so honest and from the big heart that when They burn the woods and put their lives at risk even to defend nature from those who mistreats with no point respecting the damage it makes to the environment that surrounds us.

I thank all the people who are part of the body of the forest for the hand they give to defend the environment in which you live, and everyone should bring them respect because of worlds there is only one and we must live all animals plants, etc. etc.

40. *This is also love*

Bo I do not know what to write today my brain has gone into retirement has no tips ideas to write, I will try to talk about my mother who has 80 years and time ago he came the stroke and does not make it to walk well and crawling his feet to Earth walk slowly With the support of a trolley. Then Friday night I took her to sleep at my house, because my brother had gone to find his fiancé, but my mother's night did not sleep for nothing every quarter of now called my wife because she ran the pee while having the catheter, for this also my wife and the two My daughters no year slept for nothing. This was repeated for two nights, then my wife couldn't make it anymore and told me to take my mum to her house and go too to sleep there at my mother's house, and so if done, for the night I gave him a sleeping pill and slept Well all night.

The next day my brother came back and I went back to sleep at my house, the night after while taking the sleeping pill my mum did not sleep at all and kept my brother awake for two nights because the sleeping pill did not work.

This morning I phoned my brother and sister and explained the situation I phoned the Doctor who advised me to change sleeping pill and so I did make the recipe for this new sleeping pill. Now hopefully this night my mom sleeps for the good of her and my brother.

This is also love.

41. Love the planet Earth

I like this world especially for varieties.

Variety of fish breeds of both freshwater and sea, variety of animals all beautiful, variety of plants herbs and flowers all gorgeous and beautiful to see, but I like even more for the variety of human races, from the Indians of America to the Chinese to the Negroes to whites etc. etc. This is the true richness of this planet not the money but the variety of races both human and any other living beings on the planet.

But the earth is also beautiful because of its difference in climate and the variety of land to be remade from deserts to the Amazon jungle, it is all so fascinating and to be admired before it destroys everything from the man for its false riches, money.

To hoard the precious things of the planet like oil, gold, stones Precious and so on, they destroy forests, peoples, land, seas and rivers, contaminated them or killing peoples where these riches are found, letting people think like them.

This planet that is all to love does not deserve this end but must be respected also because if the climate changes more than so comes the destruction of immense areas of land with cyclones, air horns, tornadoes and gusts of strong winds.

We hope that the planet does not rebel any longer, going to whet the rules that command the climate.

We hope that in a recent future the man will set himself in

the head to restore the damage done, especially with the deforestation that has been there, this is the first thing to do reforest deforested lands.

Another thing to do urgently is to minimize greenhouse gases to avoid overheating of the planet will be trouble.

42. *Gives it*

Women if they didn't have to be invented.

So sweet and loving you fill the heart of joy only by having them in song, even more so if this lasts for a lifetime.

So delicate when they wait for a child to come from their stomach and it is an indescribable joy for a pope, the less evil that there are women who give you so much affection if you are his companion, I regret so much when you hear that they have been raped or Beaten by your companion or even worse when your companion kills you because you left or jealous, it is a tragedy that should not exist.

Women, that the one you marry is always the most beautiful

of all, because you see her with the eyes of the love you have for her.

Women who if they are not loyal to their companion or vice versa in the house enters despair for one or the other and often breaks that magic thread that is love, suffering is very high and happens that from the times the couple leaves with great sorrow for both.

Instead when there is harmony in a couple pass the years and you seem to be married yesterday for the great love that is between both.

Marrying my wife is the most beautiful thing I've ever had in my entire life.

43. *The Dogs*

How much love they give the dogs
to their masters, they are ready to
die for his master or to save you if
you are in danger, they are jealous
of their master and do everything to
make themselves loved.

I took a canine to the kennel
where they collect the dogs
abandoned by their hosts in a kennel
here in Casentino. This canine when
we took her home we realized that
she was deaf but we kept it too, it's
so amorous she rips the caresses of
her hand and we want him so well
to the point of letting her sleep in
the room with us and puts on the
blankets at the bottom of the feet.

How much love can give a
dog to their masters I do not know,
but a dog that has been abandoned

gives him so much love when he is in a family who loves him well even if he is deaf and now even Czech from an eye cause of age Advanced.

We do not know exactly the years that has our canine but it is quite old though to a very big heart because it loves us all and it does fill with cuddles and is very amorous.

I recommend everyone to take a dog to the kennel of abandoned dogs, there are so many races and even from and puppies, surely you do a good work and you will save a dog from the safe death, I wish you to find yourself well in taking the dog as I found myself with the M The canine (Lola), and if it also has some flaws can also be a merit.

I wish you good luck if you adopt any of these dogs.

44. *Help me Jesus*

Jesus help me to love all that is good and evil on this planet.

Jesus help me with what I write to change people and let him open his heart to love for everything he creates.

Jesus help me forgive all those who are angry at me.

Jesus the first of all forgive me for all the sins I have made in my life that are so many, the first of all let me forgive from the birds that I killed when I went hunting free animals to which I removed my life.

Jesus help me to forgive me for all the wood I have worked in my life, causing the death of countless free trees in the forests.

Jesus help me to forgive me from all the people who either

offended or I treated badly and I was not able to Ask him for his forgiveness.

Jesus help me to make me love by all the people I know even if I am a little blockhead and I do not bring respect some times to the others.

Jesus help me to make people love all that is there and that exists on this planet and that must be respected because of worlds there is only one and we have the right to live all animals, trees, insects etc. etc. and also the man who is the master of the whole world.

Help me Jesus with this which I have written to cease the wars and human selfishness to which we take all the others.

45. *The winter*

It is winter and the snow has covered all the lawns and roofs of the houses in a kind of whipped cream, outside is cold is hanging in the house at the warm of the stove is pleasing.

The animals in the woods are fed with hay presses so as not to starve them to the forest or the mountain community, otherwise they would not know where to eating when the snow is too high.

Caring for wild animals is a good thing and it's a pleasure for someone to take care of it so lovingly.

The snow that when it falls does not make you wake up in the morning and find everything whitewashed, who is worse than all are the sedentary birds who can not find the food because it is under this and if the snow lasts several days some birds die of hunger , of them does not occupy anyone except some private of good heart that to eat under the huts built in mail for them.

The winter goes on and along with the snow comes the freezing very dreaded by the motorists, and starts in the streets a go and come of snow thrower and strewn salt to keep them clean and safer.

It is the month of skiers who enjoy skiing on the snow-covered slopes, being careful not to get hurt without recklessly skiing.

46. *Ecology*

I am just a passenger on this land spaceship, a passenger as one of the millions of men who inhabit this world, one that does not count anything and has no voice in anything because I am mad, discarded by the society of the healthy people.

The world I dream of is a world that those who command the government have another aspiration instead to make money or reign as a dictator, but to love their people, to love their own land and protect it from those who make it a bad use, as contaminated it with residues of all kinds.

The land in which we live is the only place in the universe in which man can live, and people must understand that there are hundreds or thousands of living animals and plants in the critical area of extinction, after which there are no more, disappeared from the earth.

For this reason a good government should recreate the appropriate environment to try to save as many species as possible from extinction, because it will be a day that we realize that we have made a splurge, run everyone behind the money printed paper and do not open the eyes to See that we are destroying our house.

People, the majority live in cities similar to large hives and do not care anything if it disappears from the world a plant to which insects and animals are connected, or collapsed an ecosystem to make way for a forestry that is only one species of tree , Beech, fir, pinewood, castagneto, forests of only oaks and Cerro, it is thus destroyed an ecosystem just because a man comes back more comfortable to have only one essence all together because so grouped is done first to work it and earn in less time more money and So They disappeared from our forest plants that today not even The imagination makes us weigh that there had been, like: The major ash is no longer, the Linden is no longer, the rate is no longer, the Mulberry and the moor are no longer there, the platinum is no longer, the Elm although C was the disease and many are Deaths there are varieties that resist the disease, but they are not reintroduced and so even they are no longer there, the horse chestnut also does not C is more, the maples outside that in the national park outside there are no more, the Holly no C is more , I could consult the books continue but that's enough, all this disappearance from our woods only depends on having made the forestry to earn more money, and destroying all the ecosystem connected to these trees, to bushes of plants that in Forestry There are no more, and animals and insects also disappear from that environment no longer having their microhabitat, so butterflies wild bees and other insects of which I do not know the name They can also extinguish themselves, and animals like the lynx, and birds like the Oriole, the Hawks, the buzzards are no longer seen, instead animals and birds that live from the waste of the man increase as, crows seagulls starlings and Crows etcetera.

For me, the destruction of the land of our country goes to the bottom of having chosen to do forestry.

47. *Winter bums Die*

The winter, in my opinion, are the saddest months even if there are Christmas parties to pull a little on the mood. Are the saddest months because with the arrival of the cold some bums die frozen in the train stations or under the footsteps of the cities, I regret so much when someone dies because they are generally good people, often find themselves so because they have lost the Work or because they are sick of some psychic illness and are not treated by doctors.

There are public dorms but not everyone goes to sleep because they are afraid that while they sleep someone also takes the little they have of money or other things, they feel safer to sleep on the street than in there.

Good people go to get them to eat and blankets when it's colder, but they can't help them all, and those most unfortunate who are not found often die of cold.

I wonder why it must be so, because those who are in the state do not think of these people who are the weakest of a nation, because they are not built of the mini apartments and data to these poor people and them also with the dress and the eating so that they do not s I find more to sleep in either the public dormitories or the street.

Loving and wanting their own people also means this to a state that only thinks for themselves and their own armchairs.

48. *Poverty*

To love the life of all living beings is the most beautiful thing in the world, especially to love the life of the weakest such as children in Africa or Brazil, or children living in orphanages around the world, which compared to children left on the street are a Little more fortunate, at least to eat they have it and the clothes as well.

I do not know more about what world you live there are rich people and others have a misery to throw away, but not only in the third world, but also here from us industrialized countries, as retirees with the least unemployed and others still that with the money they take they don't make it to pay All rent light water gas taxes of all kinds, and more and more often if they do not pay the rent they find themselves on the street to beg or accommodated by some relative or friend of good heart.

But that's not fair, this Rich people who manage all the resources of the planet has in hand all the power to enrich themselves as they seem and do not care about it if there are millions of poor something in this industrial society does not go.

Instead of a social policy where salaries between managers and workers almost equal here instead we have high salaries for managers and minimum salaries for workers, so it is not right, you have to change something that I do not even know explain.

But that's not fair.

49. What you have in your heart

You soldier wonder what you have in your heart to kill enemies, but enemies of those who might be yours, or others.

To you murderous wonder what you have in your heart when you kill another person many times you know in life, is your enemy, or a loved one of the family.

To you thief wonder what you have in your heart when you take the things that belong to others.

To you hunter wonder what you have in your heart when you take life to another living being, it was your enemy or you kill him for sports without needing to eat.

To you fisherman wonder what you have in your heart when

you fish prunes and many of them to throw again in the sea, dead , you could not try to raise them without so having unnecessary deaths.

To you lumberjack wonder what you have In the heart when you take away the life of a tree that has not so many years, that has not lived his life as other living beings but is still small only good to make us firewood to burn.

I ask you priest what you have in your heart when you give your love to everyone, as long as they ask you and you never waste it.

You doctor wonder what you have in your heart when you help another person not to die but to be cured and saved from death.

To you veterinarian I ask what you have in your heart in saving an animal from death often procured by hunters.

To you Jesus wonder what you have in the heart that you have given your life to save from sins all people as long as you repent of what year done, for your great love for all your friends.

50. *Pregnant women*

A cheer for all pregnant women, they are so sweet when they wait for a child and they are so tender, they also make happy those who watch them.

I say to all women never aborted is a pity that you will never forget, even if you stay alone because your companion has left you or because it was an occasional report I would advise you never to abort because whoever you bring in your lap is always a human life , and think about how many couples would like a child but they can't have it.

A child born is a joy for all the people who love you, and seeing him grow day after day fills the heart of joy for those who are singing and also for you.

God help you when you stay alone because nobody wants you to remember Always that you bring another person who has the right to stay in the world even when it seems to you that everything goes on the contrary never give up on putting a child in the world that will always be your greatest treasure of anything.

An appeal to all women raped who then remain pregnant please never abort, whatever if you just do not want this child, let it be born and then give it in adoption, but never kill a person who is part of you.

51. *My family*

My family consists of:

I Antonio that I am the father, my wife Mary the mother, then my eldest daughter Clare and my daughter just smaller than the first Barbara.

We also have a dog named Lola that we have taken to the kennel already large of five six years and is deaf and Czech by one eye however has a heart so great that he bought us all. The night to sleep Lola goes to bed first with my wife and Barbara then if she finds the door open comes to me or by Clare, we all want a great good.

My wife Maria is her who commands in the house, cleans and eats and taught the two daughters to keep clean and tidy in the rooms where they sleep, in short they are two good girls to whom I love him so much because besides being good I am also my Future in the world.

My wife is great to whom I want a lot of good, knows how to cook well and I am a good fork I appreciate what I cook and I always do beautiful mouthful, but now I have put on a diet and so I touch eat a little less and goodbye to the blow out.

I with the disease that I do not do almost anything, but now I'm a little better and I can water the flowers and bring the wood in the house that we need to heat the house and to eat on the thermo kitchen.

Anyway I give a hug to my whole family and I wish them all so much good.

52. *Carbonic anhydrous*

I am in love with this planet Earth, I like the animals that are there, I like the trees and flowers that are there, I also like the insects that inhabit you, the mushrooms that those that are good to eat are delicious, the fish that we are in the sea and in freshwater of The whole world are wonderful to see. I mean, I like the whole life on this planet.

But today there is a very big problem, the pollution of both the earth and the air that is perhaps also the most important, because we all breathe, and perhaps there is no remedy to stop this air pollution, due to the increase of carbon dioxide, Plants do not make it anymore to transform carbon dioxide into oxygen, already now there is the greenhouse effect in the planet with the increase in heat in World, and with the increase of automobiles and other motor vehicles, plus the plants that burn oil to produce electricity, the carbon dioxide will surely increase and the air we breathe is increasingly poorer than oxygen, hopefully in the future of A few tens of years we will not have to travel with an oxygen cylinder behind the shoulders to breathe.

The remedy there is, planting more trees and decreasing the emission of carbon dioxide into the air, building less cars, and completely shutting down the plants that produce carbon anhydrous and increase wind and photovoltaic energy, and we hope to make time to Solve the problem that is not too late.

However we do not forget
that the trees the oxygen give us
free as long as we love them.

53. *I cry in the Desert of Souls*

Jesus what do you want from me, I am just one who cries out in this desert of souls, and I Say you love this planet because it is our home, our life because everything we do comes from our planet Earth and as such must be respected and loved because it gives us life to us and to All living beings on this planet, from which we nourish ourselves and make our homes, even if our real home is not those four walls that night surround us, but our real home is out in the open air in the fields in the forests , this is our real home and as such we must feel it and of all and we have to protect it from those who want to pollute it with whatever it is.

I cry only protect the Earth Protect the air we breathe, because the air is of all and not of those who pollute it day after day with the exhaust pipe of the cars, or of the power plants that burn the oil or methane or coal fossil, and with their burn they increase in the air Carbonic anhydrous thus causing the greenhouse effect. I am only one who cries out we are careful to tease the rules that command the climate to not find one day with new deserts and other areas drowned by water. In short, I say one thing that the earth and the air belong to everyone and not to the owner of the moment that is alive, and so the earth must be defended by all those who make a bad use of the owner or not. Because the planet is all.

54. The man master of the world.

The Master Man of the world is always ready to justify himself for every crime done to nature, destroying or polluting entire plots of land in the name of progress, destroying whole ecosystems, armed with chainsaws scrapers and Diggers models the land to its own Liking, landfilling radioactive waste or other chemical poisons scrap of any chemical industry, forgetting that all these substances end up in the aquifers that brought with the Wells artesian on the surface, the water will end up being used for Irrigate the fields for our crops and so we find the poison in our dishes or even worse we find them in the drinking water that must be treated with other substances Chemicals for us in our house taps.

The man who with his intelligence has succeeded in inventing bombs so powerful as to destroy our planet many times, and in this planet there are people who still die of hunger, and other diseases that the white man has solved the problem for some time but since these People who die of hunger and diseases are poor they let themselves die, as if only wealth and weapons count on this planet and not the human sense of brotherhood even for the poorest people on the planet, so they can die surely no one will help them because they do not Year money waste printed and power with atomic bombs.

55. *Love in a couple*

What a beautiful thing when in a family there is love peace, quiet, do not raise the voice ever, but only kind and respectful words, just so respect because if there is no respect there can be no love. Every word dictated aloud, every word said with contempt, offending your companion or company makes you lose that sweet thread that is love and maybe that's precisely why many couples then leave, they leave because they lack a good education to want to bring Compared to all people and try to get along with everyone and by all means.

This is the true love of wanting to get along with all the means.

The love between two people is nice especially when you want it well, and take your company or companion for what is merits and defects included Without having to change them to your liking, but love you so for what we are.

If one seeks love just leave the open heart to accept the defects or the merits of other people and will see that love is closer than you think. Many stand alone in life and do not know what they are lost, because apart from the physical love, it is much nicer to be close to another person, to exchange two words

Say boobs and two that you want well, that we love and other kind words, this is the real sense of love between two people. And try not to quarrel ever.

56. *Letter to the Pope*

Dear Jesus, I humbly ask you the forgiveness of all my sins that I have committed in my life I know that you have committed many but the most serious are surely those made against our planet, killing animals especially free birds without committing any sin Only to be free animals in the sky and I went hunting for sports. By making the carpenter I have removed my life to many trees with the excuse of progress and the vanity of the man, trees free in the forests around the world. And as long as the man does not understand that the greatest sins are those made to our planet, our planet will rebel against our way of life. I thank God that when I had the delirium I always grumbled telling me that I was naughty and so taught me to love, love all that is good On this planet, thank God.

I thank Jesus for giving us a pope as good as it is Pope Francis and we hope that so much and healthy fields, thanks Jesus.

I remind you of your holiness that you remembered in your prayers of all the sick of any illness, even of the mentally ill who even if you do not see outward internally you suffer a lot. I thank His Holiness for his thoughts towards all the sick.

I pray His Holiness to speak to the weakest beings on the planet the trees, that without them there would be no life on this planet because they offer oxygen for free as long as we love them, and offer us another service consuming carbonic anhydrous. But today it is no longer enough to consume all the carbonic anhydrous produced by man, for this in the world there is the greenhouse effect caused by Too much carbonic anhydrous. If you will continue to cut trees and produce from the most anhydrous carbonic man there will be the end of life on this planet, because there will be no more oxygen to breathe.

His Holiness please again to spend a word on these helpless beings that give us so much, give us life.

57. *Our shop*

My wife Mari and I all two
lovers of plants and flowers we had
opened a flower shop in a country
quite close to our house, the name
of the country is Bibbiena about ten
miles from our house, but cause the
rent too high , causing the economic
crisis that struck Italy and all of
Europe, did not earn money points,
and so after about six months that
business did not go well we touched
with great displeasure close the
shop.

This shop that had been made
was beautiful furniture as I used to
do the carpenter I had all made by
me, all of maple wood then a light
wood, the counter made to her with
a large inlay made of rhombus in

the middle and with three strips on the two outer parts , two of darker woods and one in the middle of reddish wood had become a beautiful counter of Support and shelves to support the flowers and plants were always maple and they had the hat rounded on the inside and were high one different from another. As a table top always for the plants they had bought themselves of very pretty wrought iron tables and chairs always matched as working at the tables, it had become as if the flower boutique was really elegant so many that they wax the people who They came to shop to stay in a nice place to spend some time, just because it was nice.

Too bad it has come an economic crisis so that we close.

58. *Plants treat us for free*

I have said so many words to save this planet to save as much plants as possible, because it is they who give us oxygen and consume the carbon dioxide produced by the man. Let's hope that these words of mine read someone who has the power to do something that in stead of cutting the plants are instead replanted, before it is too late that the plants do not make it anymore to absorb all the carbon dioxide produced by the man. The plants in this planet will be thousands and thousands of varieties, just yesterday or heard on television that the cinnamon that the finer thickness is the most valuable because it removed the peel from the smaller plants, is an excellent natural antibiotic better than That made by the man and It is used when the antibiotic made by the man does not make it to cure the diseases.

Even aspirin was discovered by a German who chewed a sprig of willow noticed that the pain he had in his mouth totally paced and so discover what is now called aspirin. Who knows how many other plants can cure man, especially those who know the indigenous people of the ' Amazon of Africa or Indonesia know them for millennia, and the white man when he arrives with his own means destroys everything without questioning whether what he does is Right or not. And so he learns nothing of the plants that can cure himself in a natural way. It is white man you still have to learn to love nature and bring him more respect.

59. *I will leave a memory*

But what I do in the world I do not know, I write for not to be forgotten after dead. What I write to someone likes, and someone else tells me to stop shooting crap, I do not know who of the two is right though I continue to write even if someone does not approve what I do. I write why, even a man who passes on this planet, and leaves nothing of if no one wrote, no masonry or artistic work, or some invention that changed the world in his way of doing it daily, or was a great statesman, or simply A great very good person in his own trade, if he is not one of these of his passage on this planet, it is as if he had never existed a man who did not leave a memory to who will come after him. And that's why I write Right or wrong that it is because if no I am worth nothing, I have done nothing important on this world that is worthwhile to be remembered, then I write for not to be forgotten in the future, to be remembered of my thoughts by my grandchildren or grandchildren who They may say, look at my great-grandfather thought these things, or even my friends to whom I gave the book can say look at this crazy Antonio seedlings thought so.

60. The Injustice

Jesus help me today I want to die, this disease never leaves me in peace the brain one day you're a little better and another day you want to die. I'm sorry for the word balls, I can't handle this disease anymore. Anyway, let's go on until I can. The writing helps me to distract me a little and to vent all the things I have inside, all the injustices that exist in this world to tell them I relapse a bit and I am ashamed to live in a state that thinks about money and power in the world , when there are people in this planet who live with a few euro a month or who is still worse living in a nation where there is war and is destroyed the house that has put a life for have or even worse he is shot against him or his Killing family, we hope that God will forgive us all of us who live in luxury and those who live in misery. I love this planet and maybe that's what makes me pull along, I love my family however I am so sorry for here countries where there is injustice and misery. But to write me free a little ' conscience and makes me feel a little better, but so much I do not solve any of these problems, I would like someone who has power to listen to my words and treasure the best words.

61. My family

I love my wife so much, I am so fond of him, she is so much in love with me, even if sometimes I do a little upset, but she is usually right. He keeps the house and the garden clean, and always working to keep it clean, is very good and I am proud to have married her. He also educated the two my little children who are very respectful with all the people and also give him hand to place the house and do food, I'm just glad to have a family so, thank you Maria.

I could not expect more in my life, a big thank you also goes to his father and his mom that the year educated so well and also thanks always to his parents that the year allowed to marry a mentally ill who is also so far , you because my wife is From Poland.

The two of my daughters want me so well, they care for me because they are very fat and so when I take something to eat I grumble and make me put it back, so at least I'm a bit on a diet hindsight I would not make it to eat less , thanks also to my two daughters.

I'm just lucky to have a family like that.

62. The guesthouse a mirage too far

When we are young we are looking for the jobs that earn more we illusion more money to bring welfare and then you throw yourself down headlong to work to make it as much as possible with the illusion that when we retire we will enjoy life.

And so life goes on to work 8 hours you can also do overtime to spend more time working, this is what you think as a young man but when you get to a certain age towards the 50 years and see what the fact at life has not served to anything because the children Do not have the usual ideas that you have, do not give the value to what you have done in life until then, you begin to think if it is worth It is worth giving you so much out to create something that is not appreciated especially by children.

And so you make the report if it was worth having thrown all your life closed in a shed to work enjoying that month of vacation and then wait for retirement as a final mirage of a life thrown into the garbage bucket.

I have come to a conclusion, it was not worth it, and then one like me who by dint of working without enjoying for nothing life there even went crazy, and after I did not make it anymore to work cause my depressive manic disease.

For this I say that life is enjoyed day after day and working only 4 hours and being able to camp family with those hours and enough

and the rest enjoy the day, because
it camps once and the pension and a
mirage too far.

63. The word

The words according to how one the USA can cause in those who listen to them a good or bad reaction or indifference. The words if spoken with love can open every heart and bring it to love of everything you want that who listens to you want to fall in love.

The words that offend other people, lead to a reaction of irritability and then bring to the quarrel.

The words you use so many to say nothing create a mental confusion in those who listen to you and do not understand well what you mean.

The words are so many in this world of different languages that to say a word you use a mountain of different vowels and consonants, and if there is no one that translates you do not understand what one means and you can interpret a word of Love in a nothing and remain indifferent.

The most beautiful words are those that the pope says who are always words of love and brotherhood, and especially because they are always words against wars or the use of weapons in any case.

The words are very beautiful even those that are said between two lovers, full of kindness and courtesy, are also beautiful because they open your heart and when you come to give you a kiss you are full of love and see the world with other eyes, eyes to love.

64. *My life*

Life for a mentally ill is not so simple, always tied to a bag of medicines to stay a little better if they ingest it in handfuls.

To talk about when I got sick my illness I have to go back to when I was five six years old when I came the first three delusions, first with my cousin Silvia with a delirium addict, I climbed into my father's van and stripped me and as agreed he had to climb to Ven her, but instead I run away going to tell her parents and mine as I behaved. I got a nice grumble from my mother and then they didn't want you to see me and Silvia again, and that's how we haven't seen her until the age of twenty-eight when I saw her twice and then or had psychosis.

Always at the age of five six years I also had the homosexual delirium that I had only in my head but nothing happened, then always at that age I also came the mystic delirium, I was in my parents ' room on the bed, I had high fever and I had come hallucinations there Sive, I saw my sister's room out of the snakes and went to my room.

At the age of fourteen I always returned the three delusions, but nothing special happened, after which I closed to Riccio and I was out little, I had no longer a social life, at eighteen years I went a bit in the disco but after little stopped to go there. The only thing I liked to do was go hunting more than for the animals killed it was a purpose to take long walks that I was doing in the meadows and in the woods that was the real fun. Then stopped to go hunting because I rincresceva kill the birds, in the Meanwhile I had been given a canine that after being hunted with her when stopped taught him to look for mushrooms but only porcini mushrooms, I had fun so much from those I found. At the age of twenty-eight years came the acute psychosis in the three delusions, addict, homosexual and mystic, as or narrated in this book, and from the hour I am no longer healed.

My hobbies were: sowing plants in the way of extinction, but when a plant dries up, I regret so much, and now so or stopped sowing them for not suffering so much when they dry one.

The latest hobby is: Writing books, the reason is to leave a memory of me to my grandchildren and relatives, even to leave a memory of me to my friends.

I think leaving a written memory is among the most beautiful that one can leave, my thoughts my illness, they will remember me based on my thoughts, what or did I in my life As for example, the birth of hundred giant sequoias scattered then throughout the Casentino and beyond, even in Poland, in short, the important and that they dry as little as possible.

65. Psychosis and Delirium

My madness began in the year 1993 in August when in Borgo Alla Collina, a village near my house there were to play the Pooh I was sitting in the kitchen in the armchair and I had to sing my brother when I began to repent of my sins , I had taken some fruit in the abandoned fields but I began to regret so much, I felt a thief and I was very distressed until I told my brother and asked him why he never told me that that way I was stealing , then I went to bed being a little cheered.

The next day she was on vacation and I was sitting under the loggia of my house in a rocking when at some point they arrived of my relatives who had been there for many years, when I saw my cousin Silvia who I liked even when I was a child The excitement went to me a thousand and I began to hear God talking in my head, and he gave me advice on how I had to behave to go out with Silvia the woman that at that time I had fallen in love. With the dopamine to a thousand chemical substance that is in our brain and is the substance of the soul, the next day I went to find where he lived, then I found them all from my grandmother and asked Silvia if he wanted to go for a turn in the car in Pratomagno replied of Yes and with L He also came to his sister so he left all three, plus my dog Mina, that I always took me behind.

Arrived in the mountains took a walk in the meadows, but I was very tired because I hadn't slept all night for the excitement that I had taken, I brought them home and saw you again the next day at my house, the Silvia had lost her glasses and so they thought that I had Taken myself, but they were actually from the My grandmother fell behind the washing machine.

I the next day I went to find them in Prato Magno but I certainly did not find them, only after about a month my grandmother find them behind the washing machine.

My cousin Silvia after they came to my house to look for glasses no longer magazine, I phoned her the next few days but my head no longer wax I was making speeches according to my delirium and she was very angry and every time I was sick I tried to call him Peggiorand Or things just until one day I decided not to call him again.

The delirium since I saw her last time was always worse God spoke to me in my brain and always gave me advice constantly did not let me reason a second and told me how to behave with other people, I was also taken a certain excitement When I was talking to a woman and it seemed to me that every Donna fell in love with me I was in a addict delirium.

Time passed by and the delirium addict became a homosexual delirium and when I saw a man I thought he wanted to do sex with me, the thing terrified me and so I went out of the shed to pray to God that helped me not to fall into temptation the thing you r Defrosts for several days was all a go and come from the shed I went out to pray and came back to work, as long as the delirium turned into a mystical delirium, I had to become the best of all to overcome even St. Francis in goodness and God who was in my head I B Rontolava always and told me that I was bad meanwhile had begun to appear the devil in the head and I had begun to terrorize myself I was afraid of all because I saw in them the devil who spoke to me through their mouth their words were changed according to My Delirium, the thing had become terrifying, I was afraid of everyone I thought that with the medicines they wanted me to give me poison so I did not accept that they wanted me to cure.

The struggle between God and the devil in my brain had become tremendous, it was enough to blow the wind and I thought it was the devil, God also grumbled when I stomped the grass because it told me that even the grass was alive a living being that you have to respect , I was looking back on the mirror for a long time, because it was a sign of vanity looking in the mirror.

The brain was thinking between God and the devil every rustling every breath that rassomigliasse the blowing of the serpent made me think that there was the devil.

When I saw the teeth of the people I was scared as if they wanted me to eat or bite and gave me a feeling like it was the devil to Mostrarmeli and he wanted to eat me.

I once saw my sister's tongue and one of our clients banging fast as they do snakes, and I thought there was the devil inside them.

I slept a few hours, three a night and snoring with my mother's breath terrified me all night because my mother thought it was the head of the Devils.

He once told me God that I was a devil too, and as such I had to crawl on the ground like a serpent, and so I threw myself to the ground and I smuovevo as they do the snakes, this because I had dismissed my canine from Roberto my nephew because in my delirium all G Animals were angels of God and with their eyes God looked at us men as we behaved in our planet Earth and so and having removed it from him I had made a big sin because I had alienated an angel from a child.

Everything that was happening to me gave me the

certainty of living in the earthly paradise with the devil who tortured my life, and God who always grumbled me and told me what I had to do or how to behave, of course being in Paradise The interview came with the Thought where you could talk to everyone but you could not command anyone and so I spoke with the thought with my canine pero I could not command anything, sometimes when I spoke with the thought to my family God told me to be silent even with the thought PE My The devil listens to you and in the evening when it was dark God sent me flash of light to warn me that the devil was listening to me my thought so I had to shut up, even with the thought, in short I was closed in a deep silence because so much I spoke with all just With thought and enough.

The terror was so much, do you realize How to see the Exorcist, just that I cero inside.

At a distance of twenty years I still remember all the psychic pain I tried and I will not go away for my whole life what I spent in those three months when I was ill.

I do not wish anyone to have a psychosis because it is very bad and the medicine is not that they work very well.

66. *Reviews*

Dr. Paolo

The key to reading the book I believe is to be sought in the mental illness of the author, the beginning of which dates back more than 20 years ago, when Antonio was 28 years old, reading the last chapter that tells those months, I confess to have finished it with moist eyes, and the Remember went to one evening of the distant October ' 93, when with Vieri Sordi I went to find him, and he was out of the house, in the car, in the company of the dog, to fight with his delusions.

I believe that Antonio is by nature a sensitive and good person, but reading with great interest the chapters of the booklet, I thought that he too as Dante must have made a journey to hell/that for him was the sickness/from where he came back wiser and even more Sensitive and capable of loving everything and all, as he says himself, and as it transpires in so many pages, where it seems to hear certain passages of the Gospel and the Canticle of the Creatures of saint Francesco.

From his Inferno he is also able to see in a clear and essential way the things of the world that in so many aspects he does not like; And here then he tells us how it should be his ideal society, founded on love and respect, and here the thought goes to some steps of "utopia" of Moro or "the City of the Sun" by T. Campanella.

A merit of the book is the immediacy with which it is written (who is cool of classical studies tells me it is called "flow of conscience"), so much so that reading you have the impression of hearing the author speak.

Dr. Paolo

Doctor Deaf

The joy and sadness are human feelings and you have to reckon with both, some people live these emotions more than others and that's what allows Antonio to express himself with the pen giving the reader moments of PROfonda intimacy.

Thanks Antonio

Doctor Deaf

The views of the psychiatric center nurses.

Beautiful book.
Congratulations is very nice.

Giulia

It's a nice book, full of hope for a better future that you start from now on.

You participate in all that is life around you. Make people feel the pain of others "those eyes looking for someone to talk" "Loneliness around a woman who dies" "The Tramps" "The Racism" "The Handicapped".

There are so many things that make you sick: it is human malice, wars, tragedies that every day happen around us all sometimes seem to crush your dreams and your hope.

But "Help me Jesus" is your strength, the desire to always look at the heart (pag. 112) and the invitation you do to all to do it... are your strength, your rebirth continues with a woman you love and loves you and your daughters to whom you have donated this Wonderful Life , though sometimes so hard.

Your conscience is helping you understand and change, but "excessive" guilt will take away your strength and do nothing. Jesus wants you to go forth renewed and with new "strength".

to Pag. 21 You say that nature is weak and fragile, and it is not so... nature is strength, it is life... If a forest is destroyed by a fire... it is reborn and everything comes back to life, from the grass, to the tree, to the flower!!!

So is our life, your life, not weak and fragile, but ready to continue.

The disease taught you love and you know how to give it to you. Do not allow anything and none of off the light that is in you. You said Ben... "God gave us the power to love" If God gave you no one can off.

And never fear that the devil will read your heart and mind... "Can not do it" only God has this power. In the Bible it is written "come closer to God and the devil will turn away from you." Often, however, the illness can make you pass bad moments from which there for there you seem not to get out of it, but a little ' the medicine, a little ' prayer (ie to speak to God As the greatest friend you have) will get you out of the tunnel to get back to the light. My mum always said that "the darkest moment of the night is always the one that precedes the dawn"... and dawn rises every day!!!

Keep writing, love your

redwoods, your loved ones. Your writings help you, but they also help those who read them.

There will be a better world, my friend, where there will be no more wars and no pain, where people like you are going to stop suffering and finally see love everywhere.

You Jeremiah 29:11 is written "the same (God) I know well the thoughts that I have towards you, to give you a future and a hope". And think, that then there will be harmony also between man, animals and nature as it is said in Isaiah. Thinking that God mint is "impossible" don't you think?

And reading your book I felt the scent of a spring that is not there but will be sure.

Fly as high as the Eagles, my friend and not be afraid of anything and accept the cold and arid seasons and their return and your Go on in this life that sometimes wants to hinder us, but can not, as you can not stop the wind or the sea.

Your sequoias know you and know that you want them to keep on living on this earth. You are their strength, they will be yours.

Giulia

Purple

A great heart, the desire to communicate its thoughts and values, the need to overcome the loneliness of the disease by sharing the most intimate problems. This emerges from the pages of the book "Society founded on Love" of dear friend Antonio.

Purple

www.ingramcontent.com/pod-product-compliance
Lightning Source LLC
Chambersburg PA
CBHW060508290526
45791CB00001B/319